About Birds

Also in the About... series

About Mammals
About Reptiles
About Amphibians
About Insects
About Fish
About Arachnids
About Crustaceans
About Mollusks

About Birds

A Guide for Children

Cathryn Sill

Illustrated by John Sill

Columbus, OH

For the One who created birds.
—*Genesis 1:21*

First published in the United States under the title ABOUT BIRDS: A GUIDE FOR CHILDREN by Cathryn Sill, illustrated By John C. Sill.

SRAonline.com

SRA

Printed in the United States of America.

Send all inquiries to:
SRA/McGraw-Hill
4400 Easton Commons
Columbus, OH 43219-6188

ISBN 978-0-07-612514-2
MHID 0-07-612514-9

8 9 10 11 12 LHN 20 19 18 17

The **McGraw-Hill** *Companies*

About Birds

Birds have feathers.

PLATE 1
Northern Cardinal

Baby birds hatch from eggs.

PLATE 2
American Robin

Some birds build nests on the ground.

Plate 3
Ovenbird

John Gill

Some build in very high places.

PLATE 4
Bald Eagle

John Gill

And some do not build a nest at all.

PLATE 5
Common Murre

John Sill

Birds travel in different ways.

PLATE 6
Canada Geese

Most birds fly,

PLATE 7
Ruby-throated Hummingbird

John Gill

but some swim,

PLATE 8
Wood Ducks

John Sill

and others run.

PLATE 9
Greater Roadrunner

John Sill

Birds may flock together

PLATE 10
Red-winged Blackbirds

or live alone.

Plate 11
Great Horned Owl

Birds use their bills to gather food.

PLATE 12

a. Magnificent Hummingbird
b. Evening Grosbeak
c. Great Blue Heron
d. Cedar Waxwing
e. Vermilion Flycatcher

a.
b.
c.
d.
e.

They sing to let other birds know how they feel.

PLATE 13
Indigo Bunting

John Gill

Birds come in all sizes.

Plate 14

Great Horned Owl, Bald Eagle, Great Blue Heron, Northern Cardinal, Indigo Bunting, Ruby-throated Hummingbird, Red-winged Blackbird, Wood Duck, Canada Goose

John Gill

Birds are important to us.

Plate 15
Backyard

Afterword

Plate 1.
Feathers protect birds from the elements. Because feathers are so light and strong, they enable birds to fly.

Plate 2.
Although all birds hatch from eggs, different species have different nesting habits.

Plate 3.
The ovenbird gets its name from its nest, a small dome-shaped structure resembling an old-fashioned oven.

Plate 4.
Many birds build nests above the ground, varying the height according to the needs of individual species.

PLATE 5.
The common murre lays its pointed pear-shaped eggs right on rocky ledges. The elongated shape of the eggs causes them to roll in a circular motion, thus preventing them from toppling off the edge.

PLATE 6.
Canada Geese are strong flyers. They are able to migrate hundreds of miles in spring and fall.

PLATE 7.
Male ruby-throated hummingbirds beat their wings around 70 times per second. Hummingbirds are able to hover and even fly backwards.

PLATE 8.
The wood duck has webbed feet that enable it to swim. It is also a strong flyer.

PLATE 9.
The greater roadrunner has been clocked running at speeds up to 20 m.p.h. They are able to fly, but do so reluctantly.

PLATE 10.
Red-winged blackbirds flock in winter for protection. But, during the nesting season, each pair has its own territory.

PLATE 11.
Many birds of prey are solitary.

PLATE 12.
Birds also use their bills to preen their feathers, build nests and defend themselves.

Plate 13.
Birds use their voices to attract mates, defend their territory and warn others of danger.

Plate 14.
The sizes of the illustrated birds are:

a. Great blue heron—length 38", wingspread 70";
b. Bald eagle—length 32", wingspread 80";
c. Great horned owl—length 20", wingspread 55";
d. Canada goose—length 16"–25", wingspread 50"–68";
e. Wood duck—length 13 1/2", wingspread 28";
f. Cardinal—length 7 3/4";
g. Red-winged blackbird—length 7 1/4";
h. Indigo bunting—length 4 1/2";
i. Ruby-throated hummingbird—length 3 3/4"

Plate 15.
Birds benefit people in many ways. They eat harmful insects, pollinate some flowers, disperse seeds, and keep rodent populations down. Observing birds brings great pleasure to many.

Fred Eldredge, Creative Image Photography

Cathryn Sill, a former elementary school teacher, is the author of the acclaimed About... series. With her husband John and her brother-in-law Ben Sill, she coauthored the popular bird-guide parodies, A Field Guide to Little-Known and Seldom-Seen Birds of North America, Another Field Guide to Little-Known and Seldom-Seen Birds of North America, and Beyond Birdwatching, all from Peachtree Publishers.

John Sill is a prize-winning and widely published wildlife artist who illustrated the About... series and coauthored the Field Guides and Beyond Birdwatching. A native of North Carolina, he holds a B.S. in Wildlife biology from North Carolina State University.

The Sills live and work in Franklin, North Carolina.